7 Chart Patterns

That Consistently Make Money

BY ED DOWNS

CEO & Founder, Nirvana Systems Inc.

TRA

SEC

Titles in the Trade Secrets Series

*"Chart patterns form because
people react to price movements
in consistent ways based mostly on
fear, greed, and herd mentality."*

— Ed Downs

This book, along with other books, is available at discounts that make it realistic to provide it as a gift to your customers, clients, and staff. For more information on these long lasting, cost effective premiums, please us at (800) 272-2855 or email us at sales@traderslibrary.com

ISBN 1-883272-61-0

Printed in the United States of America.

1 2 3 4 5 6 7 8 9 0

Contents

Preface

There are two camps in the trading and investing world: *Fundamental Analysis* and *Technical Analysis.* If you are investing with "fundamentals," you will be interested in a company's balance sheet, product focus, and other prospects for earnings growth.

Fundamentals work great, but the problem is, *which fundamentals?* Stocks with astronomic price to earnings ratios, like Amazon, keep going higher. Stocks with bad news but sound books and products go down. Trading with such information is just downright hard — especially when the market isn't going up.

Since the day I first started trading some 20 years ago, I've been fascinated and awed by the power of Technical Analysis and Charting. According to my studies and from talking with Nirvana customers, successful traders use technical methods — almost exclusively. Chart patterns work! Why? Because human behavior repeats itself. There are two forces at work: greed and fear. What you see in charts is the transition between investor elation and terror.

Seven Chart Patterns That Consistently Make Money is purposely not a long book. I have seen chart books that went on and on for 200 pages or more. You don't need that much information. After studying the markets for 20+ years, I have come down to these seven patterns as the key predictors of direction, in any market.

We use our product, OmniTrader, to prospect for trading candidates, but it doesn't matter what method you are using — if you confirm your entries with these simple patterns, you will be light-years ahead of the average investor. Best of luck in all your trading endeavors.

— Ed Downs

7 Chart Patterns

That Consistently Make Money

Introduction

DIFFERENT CHARTS AND HOW TO READ THEM

Before the personal computer revolution of the 80s, technical analysis or charting was considered a black art. Today, financial news commentators often turn to their favorite market technician to find out what the charts are "saying." The reason? Charts work! But before we discuss charts, we should cover a few basics about how charts are displayed. Price charts are typically drawn in one of three styles: a bar chart, a candle chart, or a line chart. Examples are shown at the right.

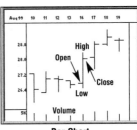

Bar Chart

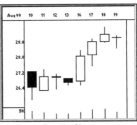

Candle Chart

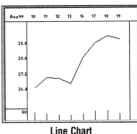

Line Chart

On each day of a security's life there are five pieces of information recorded:
- The Open—the price the market opened at the beginning of the day
- The High—the highest price reached during the day
- The Low—the lowest price reached

- The Close — the final price
- Volume — the number of shares which changed hands

Each price bar is represented as a vertical line from the high to low. Small lines point left and right, which are the open and close, respectively. Volume is almost always shown as a line below the bar.

In a candle chart, the range between the open and close is shown as a rectangle, or body. If the day closed "up," the body is hollow. If the day closed "down," the body is typically filled in. A line chart is just a line connecting closing prices. This type of chart is rarely used by technical analysts. In this book, we will use candle charts where the timeframe is not too compressed. Otherwise, we will show a bar chart for ease of viewing.

Chapter 1

THE POWER OF TECHNICAL ANALYSIS

Trading vs. Investing: Choose One and Profit From It

At the dawn of the bull market in the 80s and early 90s, the best approach for any investor was clearly "buy and hold." With interest rates low and the stock market advancing slowly and steadily, one could earn a nice return on his or her "nest egg" by just socking money away in a mutual fund and letting it ride.

The playing field has changed. We now have a Dow over 10,000 (see Figure 1-1) and a volatile NASDAQ that can gain and lose 2%-5% on any given day. Internet stocks are tripling in value in a matter of weeks, only to be thrashed when earnings don't materialize. It's an amazingly volatile time. The good news is that volatility can lead to huge profits if taken advantage of properly.

Most traders start out as investors. Maybe they had some money socked away in a 401K plan, and saw the opportunities in "dot com" and "high tech" stocks, realizing that if they had invested in these stocks, they would have made huge gains in a very short time. The budding trader starts by calling a discount broker, setting up an account, and buying some shares of Amazon, Intel, or Dell Computer stocks.

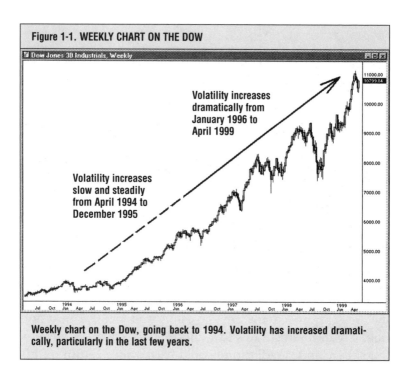

Figure 1-1. WEEKLY CHART ON THE DOW

Dow Jones 30 Industrials, Weekly

Volatility increases
dramatically from
January 1996 to
April 1999

Volatility increases
slow and steadily
from April 1994 to
December 1995

Weekly chart on the Dow, going back to 1994. Volatility has increased dramatically, particularly in the last few years.

But then, they find that the stock that was going up, suddenly takes a nosedive. Instead of making a boring 2% gain for the month, they realize a 20% loss. Ouch! Maybe they should have watched the market more closely. They start reading about different methods, Internet resources, and other ideas for determining what is going up and what is going down. And, after a while, they begin to realize that the best and simplest way to figure out what is going up, and what down, is to use technical analysis, or charting.

The following charts illustrate the potential difference between trading and investing. On the next page (see Figure 1-2), we have a chart of stock Ethan Allen (ETH) for one year, from January 1998 to January 1999. If we had purchased ETH at the start of 1998 and held for one year, we would have realized a 13% gain. Not bad.

Figure 1-2. BUY AND HOLD — INVESTING

13% gain in one year.

Buy and hold gain of 13% in one year.

Now, let's consider what could have happened had we traded the moves in this stock (see Figure 1-3). By going long (buying the stock) in early January 1998 and selling it in April, we would have made a 45% gain. Then, by shorting the stock[1] and making money as it declined, we would have picked up another 46%. Finally, a purchase of the stock again in early October would have yielded a very nice 68% gain through January 1999.

The gains were calculated by dividing the point movement by the price at the start of the move. By adding up the total percentage of gain on each trade, we ended up

───────────────

1 See "The Power of the Short Side" on page 20.

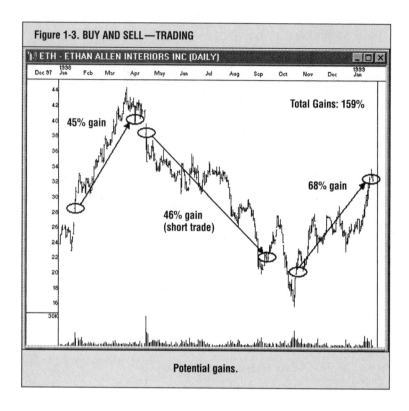

Figure 1-3. BUY AND SELL—TRADING

ETH - ETHAN ALLEN INTERIORS INC (DAILY)

Total Gains: 159%

45% gain

68% gain

46% gain
(short trade)

Potential gains.

with over *ten times* the "buy and hold" gain — netting a hefty 159% gain.

Strategy	Total Gains
Buy and Hold	13%
Trading	45% + 46% + 68% = 159%

The key to this performance is staying in the market and making steady, consistent gains. While it is true that commission costs are incurred from trading, modern discount brokerages charge as little as $7 to execute a trade. In the above example, we had three trades which would have incurred six brokerage commissions (one each to buy and sell), giving us a cost of $42. If you had invested $5,000 trading this stock, you would have ended up with $12,950 in the account for a gain of $7,950. The $42 cost is negligible.

A Sneak Preview of What You Will Learn:

The questions are: "How do we find the trades?" and "How do we know when to buy and sell?" Glad you asked. Each of the "entry points" and "exit points" which were marked in Figure 1-3 by the oval circles, exhibits a pattern you will learn about in Chapters 2-11, and are also illustrated below (see Figure 1-4). This will seem like Greek to you now. But, after you have finished studying the material, you will want to come back and examine this chart.

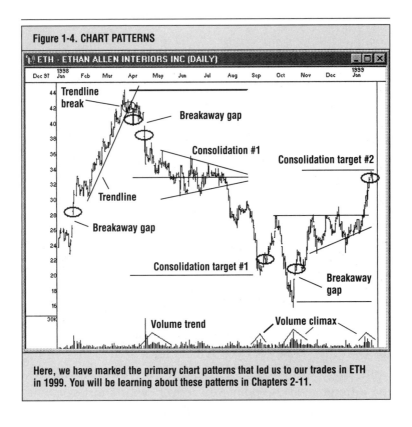

Figure 1-4. CHART PATTERNS

Here, we have marked the primary chart patterns that led us to our trades in ETH in 1999. You will be learning about these patterns in Chapters 2-11.

The Power of the Short Side

If you have never shorted a stock, that's OK. In fact, if you have no idea what "shorting" is, that's fine too. In our experience, only 2% of the investing public are aware of the short side. But, it's an extremely profitable technique, and something you will want to understand thoroughly—and apply.

What Is Short Selling?

Let's explain by way of example. Suppose your uncle entrusted you with his Mercedes for the summer. He heads for the Bahamas and says, "I'll see you in the fall." At that time, Mercedes are in short supply, and the going rate is about $30,000 to own this fine automobile.

Unknown to your uncle, you sell his car and put the money in your bank account, earning interest. Now, come August, the Mercedes supply problem has been solved, so there are more of them on the market. You go out and buy the Mercedes back for $25,000. Your uncle returns, gets his car, and you pocket $5,000.

That's how short selling works—you borrow stock from your broker (owned by somebody else) and sell it to the market. You owe the broker the stock. Later, you hope to buy it back (from the market) and replenish the stock you borrowed. If it is priced lower at that point, you pocket the difference.

However, what happens if the item is pricier in the future? Let's say that there is a sudden run on Mercedes in early August, and it costs you $35,000 to buy one. You must come up with this money, so you will suffer a $5,000 loss. In the same way, if you short stock and it goes up, you will lose the difference at the point you "cover" your short sale.

Why Sell Short?

Notice how steep the declines were, versus the rallies, in the chart below (see Figure 1-5). The truth is stocks and futures fall much faster than they rise. Why? Because fear is a stronger emotion than hope. It takes less energy for people to buy into a rally than to sell into a panic. If your favorite stock is going up, you aren't very likely to buy more, even if you think it's going higher.

If a security is falling like a rock, the emotion is, "Get out!" So, thousands of players will sell at the same time to avoid taking a loss. By and large, investors and funds are "long," meaning they own the stock. So, there is a huge wall of

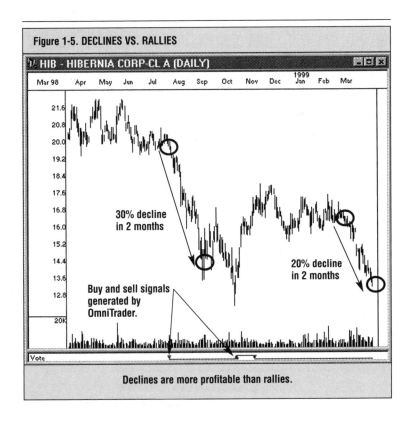

Figure 1-5. DECLINES VS. RALLIES

HIB - HIBERNIA CORP-CL A (DAILY)

30% decline in 2 months

20% decline in 2 months

Buy and sell signals generated by OmniTrader.

Declines are more profitable than rallies.

pent-up selling pressure, just waiting to be unleashed anytime bad news enters the market.

Selling short is something every trader should do. The market has ebbs and flows. And, ferocious declines happen often, typically once a quarter. On a smaller scale, they happen every day to certain issues and contracts (futures). Trading the short side is a very profitable habit.

Below (see Figure 1-6), we see another great example of a short trade that made big money. In early April of 1999, Pfizer, Inc. (PFE) had a breakaway gap down, and broke a trendline. You are going to be reading about both these patterns soon!

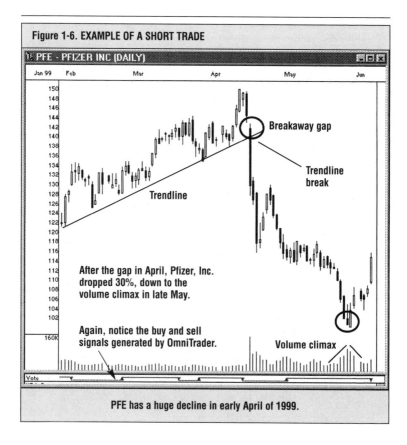

Figure 1-6. EXAMPLE OF A SHORT TRADE

PFE has a huge decline in early April of 1999.

Look again at the chart and analyze what happened. On April 15, the stock plummeted from 144 to 129 in one trading session. If you had gone short on April 14, you would have realized a gain of 10%, in ONE DAY! If you had held your short position in this stock until the volume climax that occurred on May 25, you would have made 25% on the trade.

You will read about gaps, trendline breaks, and volume climaxes in the next eight chapters. After you have read Chapters 2-9, come back to this chart and the patterns will be much more obvious. One more note—you can see buy and sell signals below the chart. These were generated by OmniTrader[2] using other technical trading systems. While having a tool like OmniTrader can help you find great candidates (like this one), the patterns we will soon study can be applied to any chart—discovered by any method.

$10,000 to $1 Million in One Year

In 1980, I came across a little book at a trading seminar called *The Profit Magic of Stock Transaction Timing,* by J.M. Hurst. This little book had a profound impact on my development as a trader.

In his book, Mr. Hurst proved two points to my satisfaction:

- Stock market movement is *not* random, and by analyzing a large "stable" of stocks using basic technical methods (he used cycles and trendlines) one could find excellent opportunities for profit each and every day.

- By keeping one's funds 100% invested at all times, it was very possible to achieve returns of 2,000% and higher through the magic of compounding.

---

2 See pages 84 and 85 for more information on OmniTrader

Back in the 60s, when Mr. Hurst wrote his book, we didn't have the volatility we have today. We are now seeing stocks that move 2%, 4%, even 10% in a single day.

And, it is possible to turbo-charge your trading through the use of margin. If you are trading on margin with your broker, you can trade *twice* your account balance. That is, if you have $10,000 in your account you can actually take $20,000 in positions in the market. So, a 1% gain in a fully margined account is like 2% in a non-margined account. By the way, the interest the broker will charge you for borrowing these funds is negligible — something like .02% per day.

If you start with $10,000 and earn just 2% a day for 250 trading days in a year, your $10,000 would grow to $1.4 million.

I started thinking, "If you actually made 2% a day (1% on margin), what would happen to an initial stake of $10,000?" I stayed up late one night and wrote a little program to calculate compound rates of return given different assumptions. Here's what I found:

If you start with $10,000 and earn just 2% a day for 250 trading days in a year, your $10,000 would grow to $1.4 million.

Again, going back to the lesson from Mr. Hurst, the trick is to stay invested at all times and make small, consistent gains. And remember, we really only need to clear 1% if we are trading on margin.

Is It Really Possible to Make 1% a Day in the Markets?

Every day a host of stocks make moves of 5% or more. One and two percent movers are everywhere. The big challenge is FINDING THE OPPORTUNITIES, and sorting or ranking them to find the best candidates.

That's why we created OmniTrader, to help us with the task of finding great trading opportunities each day in the market. The next chart (see Figure 1-7) shows two signals from OmniTrader Real Time. One chart had a buy signal with a beakaway gap, and the other had a sell confirmed by a trendline break—at the same time. You would have made money on both charts—the one on the left by taking a short position. Both trades exceeded our 1% per day requirement, after deducting the spread between the bid and ask, and also deducting a typical $8-$12 commission.

Can you see the sheer power of today's markets? How many investors are aware of this? After reading this book, 30% a year is going to seem very boring. The point is, these moves are everywhere. And, the market gives us great confirming chart patterns every day, on thousands of opportunities!

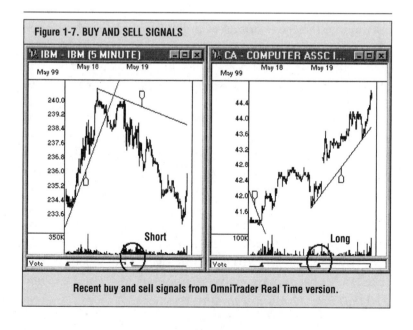

Figure 1-7. BUY AND SELL SIGNALS

Recent buy and sell signals from OmniTrader Real Time version.

The Power of Compound Gains

If you can make 2% a week in a margined account, fully invested with compound gains, the account will increase by more than *seven times* (768%) in one year.

Gain per Week:	Account After One Year:	Total Gain (%)
1%	$28,000	280%
2%	$76,865	768%
3%	$206,968	2,069%
5%	$1,420,429	14,204%

Total gains on 50% margin, with profits compounded.

Do Technical Analysis and Charting Work?

The clear answer to the question, "Can Technical Analysis and Charting make me money?" is, "Yes!" There are many documented success stories of individuals who win big year after year, using technical trading methods exclusively. The best sources are the books *Market Wizards* and *The New Market Wizards* (available from traderslibrary.com).

These interviews with great traders will both inspire and educate you. Read about Ed Seykota, who multiplied his clients' accounts by 2500 *times* (250,000%) in about ten years. Then there's Michael Marcus, who parlayed a $30,000 initial stake into *$80 million.*

Another famous trader, not included in Jack's book, is Larry Williams, who won a national trading competition in 1987 by multiplying $10,000 into over $1,000,000 *in one year.* He subsequently wrote a book titled, *How I Turned $10,000 Into $1 Million in One Year.*

Each of these traders said they use technical methods, almost exclusively. Did these gentlemen discover the secret to riches? Not according to them. If you read the interviews, you will find that each trader said basically the same thing: develop a trading system that matches your trading style, and maintain discipline in sticking to your system.

The Formula for Success in Trading

Every successful trader develops a trading style that matches his or her personality. You, too, have a natural inclination towards your own, personal style. And whatever your style, it is important that your trading match it. You may be very short-term oriented, wanting to capitalize on quick, five-to-ten day moves to make many small profits over a long period of time. If you are less active or more sensitive to commission costs, you may want to trade every six weeks or so, and to set wide stops so that your trades have breathing room.

The Formula for Success in Trading:

1 Find a trading style that matches your personality.

2 Develop a system according to the trading style.

3 Stick to the system (discipline).

You may want to focus on the general market trend, or may feel more confident trading short-term opportunities against the trend. Almost any method will work, if it matches your personality and incorporates good money management principles. Van K. Tharp, one of the traders interviewed by Schwagger for *Market Wizards*, has since written the book *Trade Your Way to Financial Freedom*, which is devoted to developing your own trading style.

▲ ▲ ▲ ▲ ▲ ▲

Summary

In Chapter 1, we have covered the following, important points as a prelude to our study of chart patterns in the markets:

- Trading is superior to investing in terms of potential gains for the same amount of time.
- Trading the short side can be *extremely* profitable.
- It is possible to make 1%-4% each and every day in the market.
- If you can make just 2% a day—or just 1% on margin—a $10,000 account will grow to *$1.4 million* in one year.

Technical Analysis and Charting work, provided you find a method or pattern that you are comfortable with, and stay with it. As you study this book, some patterns will "jump out at you" as being totally obvious. Focus on those. As a great trader once said, "You only need one pattern to be successful."[3]

With this background behind us, we're ready to dive right into our main topic—the seven chart patterns for successful trading! These patterns have proven themselves over and over to be tremendous predictors of tomorrow's market, and the individual stocks and futures that comprise it.

---

3 Linda Bradford Raschke, *The New Market Wizards*

Chapter 2

THE SEVEN CHART PATTERNS FOR SUCCESSFUL TRADING

Computers Can't See Everything

The computer is great at performing mathematical and numerical comparisons. The entire field of technical analysis since 1980 has been enhanced and powered by the fact that machines can run indicators and systems quickly, freeing the technician for higher-level tasks. And there are a lot of computerized trading systems available.

The various technical analysis and charting programs available — MetaStock, TradeStation, and OmniTrader, can help you find opportunities faster. That is their value. But, once you get a candidate, you can very quickly look at it and determine whether it is a prime candidate by measuring how much "force" there is behind the stock to make it move, as indicated by its "chart pattern."

Chart patterns are simply interpretations of different price formations and their implications for the future of a stock. The ability to recognize and identify successful chart patterns is the key for highly effective trading.

Chart Patterns

In my 20 years of charting experience, I have distilled the most successful "chart patterns" down to the following seven (see Figure 2-1). These patterns are classified into two basic types: momentum (breakout) and exhaustion (reversal).

By the term breakout we mean measuring situations where a security has or is acquiring momentum, meaning it will move further in a given direction. Patterns which fall in this category have an X in the "B" column. By reversal we mean detecting that a move is ending, so we can avoid getting in at just the wrong time — or, trade in the other direction. These patterns are marked under "R."

Figure 2-1. SEVEN CHART PATTERNS FOR SUCCESS			
#	**CHART PATTERN**	**B**	**R**
1	Support and Resistance	X	X
2	Trendline Break and Reversal	X	X
3	Saucer Formations	X	
4	Fibonacci Retracements		X
5	Price Gaps	X	X
6	Volume Climax and Volume Trend	X	X
7	Consolidations	X	
The seven chart patterns are classified as either breakout (B) or reversal (R) type patterns, or both.			

Chapters 3-9 cover these chart patterns, starting with Support and Resistance, which can serve as either a breakout or reversal type of pattern.

Chapter 3

CHART PATTERN 1: SUPPORT AND RESISTANCE

Support and resistance have been used for a very long time by technicians and anyone who watches markets—even fundamentalists! Support is a level or area on the chart under the market where buying interest is sufficiently strong to overcome selling pressure. As a result, a decline is halted and prices turn back up again. A support level is usually identified beforehand by a previous reaction low or trough. Resistance is the opposite of support and represents a price level or area over the market where selling pressure overcomes buying pressure and a price advance is turned back. A resistance level is usually identified by a previous peak.

> **A support level is usually identified beforehand by a previous reaction low or trough.**
>
> **A resistance level is usually identified by a previous peak.**

When a solid support level forms, the psychology of this level becomes more important the more times price approaches it and retreats. More buying will continue to come into the security because the participants expect price to reverse off the line (see Figure 3-1), and try to anticipate it.

The chart for General Motors (GM) shows important support and resistance breaks (see Figure 3-2). It is often difficult to determine whether a support level will hold or be broken. That is why we are discussing this pattern first — it is the weakest and most difficult to use.

However, when you see a clear support line form, and it is broken, that usually means price will continue down lower. If it bounces off the level, it will likely continue high-

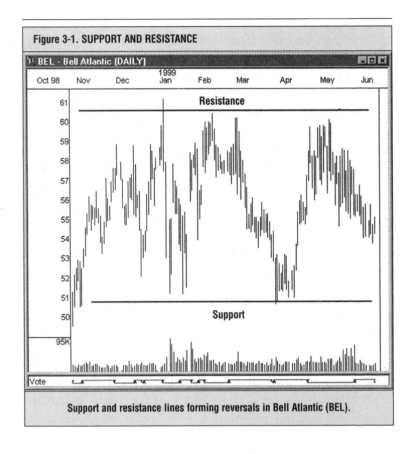

Figure 3-1. SUPPORT AND RESISTANCE

Support and resistance lines forming reversals in Bell Atlantic (BEL).

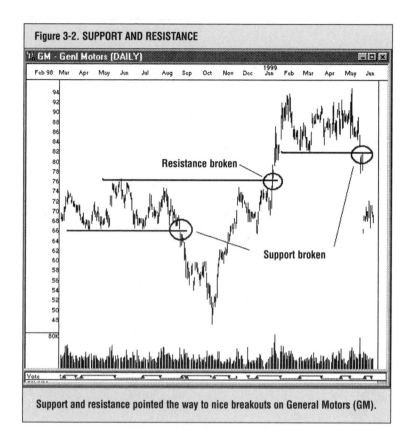

Figure 3-2. SUPPORT AND RESISTANCE

GM - Genl Motors (DAILY)

Resistance broken

Support broken

Support and resistance pointed the way to nice breakouts on General Motors (GM).

er. When looking for a support break, you want to see major strength — such as a gap or heavy volume accompanying the break.

Chapter 4

CHART PATTERN 2: TRENDLINE BREAK AND REVERSAL

Trendlines are perhaps the oldest tools known to chartists. Trendlines form across peaks and valleys called pivot points—relative highs and lows in a chart. As more points form along a line, it becomes more "established." This means that, when the line is broken, it will likely follow through with a strong move in the new direction.

> **Trendlines form across peaks and valleys called pivot points—relative highs and lows in a chart. As more points form along a line, it becomes more "established."**

After a trendline has formed, we look for reversals when price moves in proximity to the trendline and pulls back, but also watch for breaks through it. Either event can be significant and predict the next price move (see Figure 4-1).

When you draw a trendline, you should be aware of the approximate cycle for the peaks and valleys. In his book *The Profit Magic of Stock Transaction Timing*, J.M. Hurst proved that stocks fall in 16, 32, and 64 period cycles (which we will call

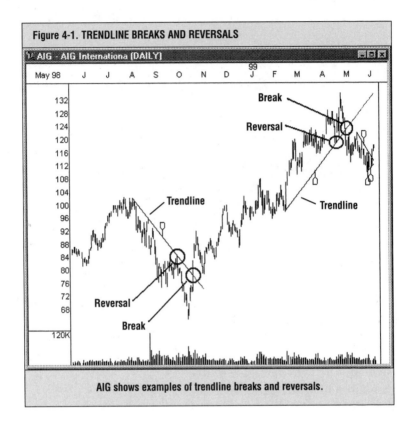

Figure 4-1. TRENDLINE BREAKS AND REVERSALS

AIG shows examples of trendline breaks and reversals.

short, medium, and long term).[4] These measurements are the approximate valley-to-valley or peak-to-peak distances in each time frame that you see a reversal (pivot point).

It is important to understand which time frame you are working when you use a trendline, because you may want to set your target exit point at approximately the halfway point. That is, if you are using a medium-term trendline, you would expect price to reach an extreme point and reverse approximately $32/2 = 16$ periods from the previous pivot.

---

4 Our experiments indicate the same cycles work on futures as well.

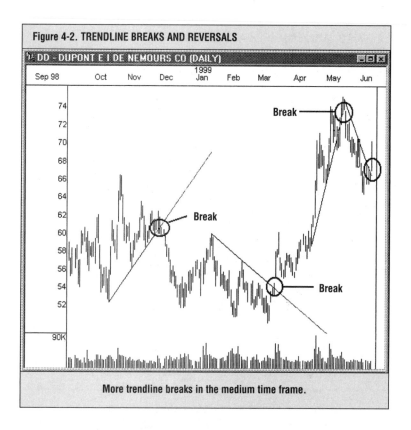

Figure 4-2. TRENDLINE BREAKS AND REVERSALS

DD - DUPONT E I DE NEMOURS CO (DAILY)

More trendline breaks in the medium time frame.

The trendlines in Figure 4-1 are based on medium-term pivots, as are the ones in the chart above (see Figure 4-2). Again, if you measure the approximate distance from peak to peak or valley to valley for each trendline, you would see about 6-7 weeks (30-35 trading days) of price action forming these cycles.

The chart (see Figure 4-3) for Air Touch Communication (ATI) shows trendline pivots in the short-term time frame. Indeed, you can see that the measurement from peak to peak or valley to valley is approximately 3-4 weeks, or about 16 trading periods. And, the next relative peak or valley is typically 7-9 periods from the previous valley or peak, respectively.

Figure 4-3. TRENDLINE BREAKS AND REVERSALS

The trendlines marked in this chart are based on short-term pivots.

One last note on trendlines — the best angle on a line for breaks is 45 degrees. The shallower the angle, the less pronounced any breaks are likely to be. Conversely, for trendline reversals, you want to see a shallow angle formed by the trendline — 20 to 30 degrees or so is best.

Chapter 5

CHART PATTERN 3:
SAUCER FORMATIONS

S aucer patterns are fairly rare, but are usually very pre-dictive. The saucer pattern shows a gradual change in trend as it develops (see Figure 5-1). It is important that the formation show a clear arc with tight trading ranges at the bottom of the arc. This pattern can be traded for short-term moves, but is much better if held for a long period of time. Set stops just below the saucer bottom (the lows of the formation). A stop is used to exit a position if a certain price level is broken. Generally, they are set below the current market price.

> **The saucer pattern shows a gradual change in trend as it develops. It is important that the formation show a clear arc with tight trading ranges at the bottom of the arc.**

In Figure 5-1 on the next page, Hunt JB Transport Services Inc (JBHT) formed a saucer bottom and rallied over the next year to double in price. Saucers can occur in short or long time frames.

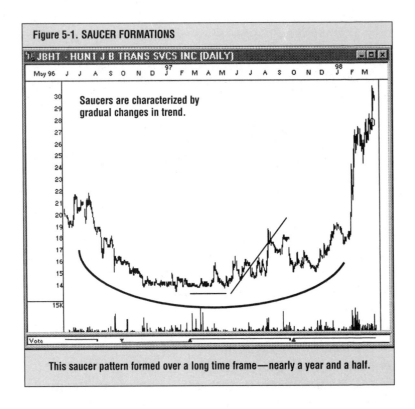

Figure 5-1. SAUCER FORMATIONS

JBHT - HUNT J B TRANS SVCS INC (DAILY)

Saucers are characterized by gradual changes in trend.

This saucer pattern formed over a long time frame—nearly a year and a half.

Another, more pronounced saucer, can be seen on the Columbia/HCA Healthcare Corp (COL) chart on the next page (see Figure 5-2). We have marked another confirming pattern, a breakaway gap, indicating the saucer has completed and the stock will rally considerably from that point.

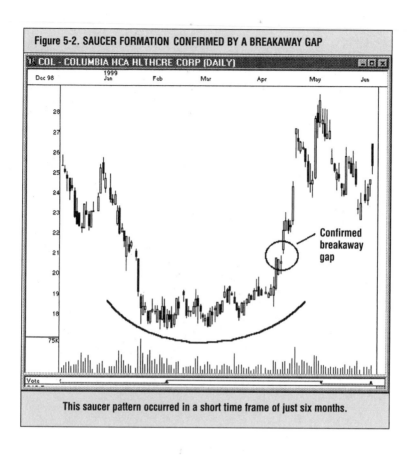

Figure 5-2. SAUCER FORMATION CONFIRMED BY A BREAKAWAY GAP

This saucer pattern occurred in a short time frame of just six months.

Chapter 6

CHART PATTERN 4: FIBONACCI RETRACEMENTS

Gann was probably the first trader to use Fibonacci retracement ratios. The Fibonacci number sequence occurs in nature frequently (1, 3, 5, 8, 13, 21, . . .). Ratios of these numbers to each other form the values 38%, 50%, and 62%. As it turns out, these are very close to the Gann numbers 3/8 (37.5%), 4/8 (50%), and 5/8 (62.5%), which he used over and over in his chart calculations.

Figure 6-1 shows 50% retracements occurring in three places. By the word "retracement" we mean price retreated from a high, to the 50% point of the prior move. You can see, for example, that in August we formed a low point for Mobile (MOB), and in September we formed a high. If you take half the distance between these two points, you get the approximate point at which price reversed in mid-November.

The Fibonacci retracement phenomenon happens over and over in markets of all kinds. Essentially, you look at the most recent significant low and high, and make measurements on a move between these points. Measure the 3/8 point (38% of the distance from the last pivot) and look for a reversal there. If it doesn't happen, move on to the 4/8 (50%) point and finally the 5/8 (62%) point.

It should be noted that the 50% retracement is the most common, followed by the 38%, and last the 62% level. That is, you should always expect a 50% retracement, but be prepared for a 38% or 62%. A good rule of thumb is to enter a trade on 50% retracement but exit a trade at 38%. This is done to preserve profits at the nearest retracement point (if we wait for 50%, we may not get it).

These methods work particularly well on the Dow and on futures contracts. It would seem that any market which is liquid (has reasonable volume) works well with this technique.

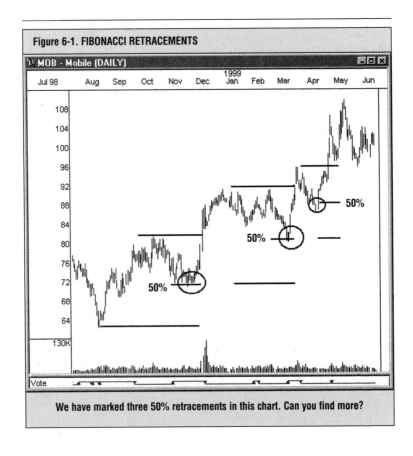

Figure 6-1. FIBONACCI RETRACEMENTS

We have marked three 50% retracements in this chart. Can you find more?

Chapter 7

CHART PATTERN 5: GAPS (BREAKAWAY, MEASURED, EXHAUSTION)

Our fifth pattern is one of my absolute favorites. Gaps are basically points of high or low demand. Usually, the pent-up buying or selling pressure that forms the gap will follow through in the general market with more buying or selling. Hence, the pattern is powerful in predicting a continuation move. There are many technical trading books that describe gaps. There are three basic kinds: breakaway gap, measured gap and exhaustion gap (see Figure 7-1).

> **Gaps are basically points of high or low demand.**

Breakaway gaps occur at the ends of moves, in the opposite direction. They are usually the most profitable and easiest to trade.

Measured gaps occur at (approximately) the 50% point of moves, and are more difficult to identify when they happen. But as price moves away in the direction of the gap, it can become apparent that the gap has likely marked the 50% point, giving us a target for the end of the move.

Finally, the exhaustion gap occurs at the end of a move. Exhaustion gaps are differentiated from measured gaps by observing what price does after the gap forms. If it reverses to move into the zone of the gap, you probably have exhaustion.

Figure 7-1 had a gap in May 1997, near the long signal shown. This served to confirm the long as a higher probability signal. These examples are taken from our product, OmniTrader. But regardless of what product you use, or how you get the initial signal, you can quickly see if you have a gap near a signal you are considering trading.

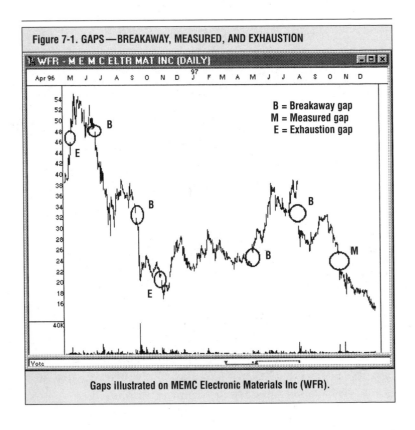

Figure 7-1. GAPS—BREAKAWAY, MEASURED, AND EXHAUSTION

Gaps illustrated on MEMC Electronic Materials Inc (WFR).

Chapter 8

CHART PATTERN 6: VOLUME CLIMAX, VOLUME TREND

Volume climaxes are beautiful patterns that are about 90% accurate in terms of predicting a reversal move tomorrow. When they occur, the market will likely move in the opposite direction — we just don't know how much.

A climax occurs when a market has been trending down (or up) for an extended period of time, usually for several months.

In this example (see Figure 8-1) of AllState Corp (ALL) you can see several great examples of volume climaxes, and several lesser ones. Particularly, the climax in late June and early August were powerful.

Volume climaxes are beautiful patterns that are about 90% accurate in terms of predicting a reversal move tomorrow. Volume trend, the inverse pattern to a volume climax, looks like a climax except the price does not retreat.

It is interesting to note that stocks (or futures) that exhibit volume climaxes typically repeat the pattern a number of

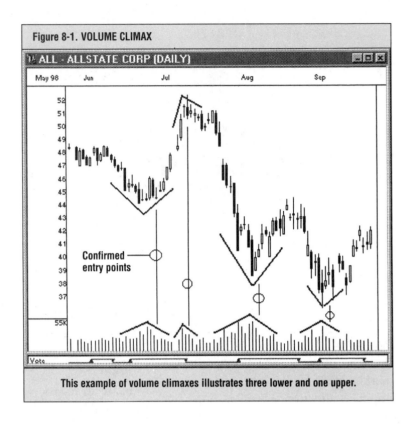

Figure 8-1. VOLUME CLIMAX

This example of volume climaxes illustrates three lower and one upper.

times. So, when you find a security that exhibits a volume climax, bookmark it and wait for the next one to form!

Volume climaxes are characterized by sudden increases in volume. Suddenly, the market moves quickly in the same direction as it was previously moving, on heavy volume. Then price retreats on lighter volume.

Volume climaxes are particularly accurate at the end of long moves, near significant market tops or bottoms, or near Fibonacci retracement points (38%, 50%, 62%).

Volume Trend Is Just as Powerful

The inverse pattern to a volume climax is called a volume trend, which looks like a climax except price does NOT retreat. That is, as the volume spike falls off, price continues in the same direction. This event indicates price will continue in the current direction, not reverse. Figure 8-2 for Office Depot (ODP) illustrates the concept with several examples. Especially, note the trend pattern that occurred in November.

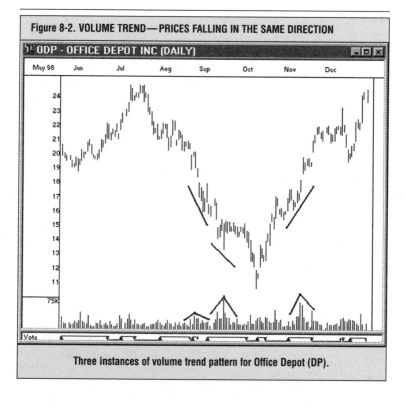

Figure 8-2. VOLUME TREND—PRICES FALLING IN THE SAME DIRECTION

Three instances of volume trend pattern for Office Depot (DP).

Chapter 9

CHART PATTERN 7: CONSOLIDATIONS (FLAGS AND TRIANGLES)

A consolidation is a place where buyers and sellers are very closely matched in numbers (see Figure 9-1). As the battle ensues, others (on the sidelines) notice that the market is consolidating, and begin considering getting on board. As soon as a breakout to the upside (or downside) occurs, the latent buyers (or sellers) usually begin taking positions. You want to look for places where price moves outside the trading range that forms the consolidation, on increasing volume.

A consolidation is the price movement in a "trading range" between two trendlines — it can appear in the formation of a triangle or a flag.

In Figure 9-1, we see several consolidations set up as the stock declines. And, we see several different kinds. The first two marked consolidations are triangles and the third and fourth are flags.

The time frame of the consolidation is used to determine the target. That is, if the consolidation lasts two weeks, you

Figure 9-1. CONSOLIDATIONS—FLAGS AND TRIANGLES

Consolidations imply a continued price move in the same direction. The first two marked consolidations are triangles and the third and fourth are flags.

should go back on the chart approximately two weeks to measure the recent high or low. The distance of the next move is also in direct proportion to the size of the consolidation.

Look at the second consolidation that started in January of 1998 and continued until about May. The approximate size of the consolidation, then, is four months. If you go back four months from the start of the consolidation, you can find a peak at that point, in the September/October time frame. And, the end of the move measured by that consolidation was about four months later, in October of 1998.

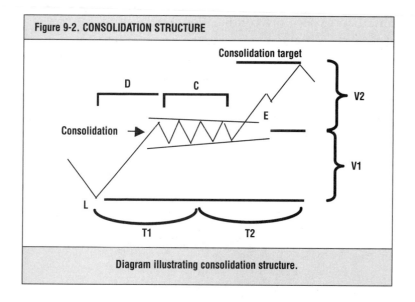

Figure 9-2. CONSOLIDATION STRUCTURE

Diagram illustrating consolidation structure.

The diagram above (see Figure 9-2) illustrates the structure which usually forms around consolidations[5]. The consolidation is shown in the middle of the drawing, representing price movement in a "trading range" between two trendlines — the definition of a consolidation. After the consolidation completes and reaches its "target," you will usually find that T1 = T2 and V1 = V2. We also usually note that the previous low, marked L, is typically found from the start of the consolidation back into the past, an amount of time equal to the width of the consolidation. That is, most consolidations form such that C = D.

As consolidations form, you want to look back on the chart to the previous, probable significant low, approximately the same distance as the width of the consolidation,

---

5 Turn this diagram upside-down for a short trade. The examples on the previous page are all shorts.

and then expect any continuation move out of the consolidation to last the same amount of time into the future. Typically, the entry point will be at E (see diagram) after the consolidation forms. By making these measurements, you can quickly assess how far the stock is likely to go from that point, by just measuring T1 and V1 and projecting T2 and V2 into the future. Look at some charts and verify this for yourself. It works.

▲ ▲ ▲ ▲ ▲ ▲

Summary

We have presented the 7 Chart Patterns in Chapters 3-9. All of these patterns can predict moves in any tradeable security (stocks, futures contracts, etc.). Just grab a chart, sit down, and start marking patterns. They will soon begin to jump out at you!

These same seven patterns can be used to predict market direction. That's exactly what I do on SignalWatch, as you will see in Chapter 10.

Chapter 10

PREDICTING MARKET
DIRECTION

echnical analysis works! I have been running my daily SignalWatch commentary since September 1998. In Chapter 10, we will look at how you can use the patterns we have discussed to predict the Dow for tomorrow.

About SignalWatch.com

SignalWatch was launched in an interesting way. We recently took on the task of educating our website designers on trading and using OmniTrader. After showing them how to use the software to pinpoint opportunities, and then read simple patterns on charts to improve odds, they suggested starting a website to help educate our customers. We implemented their suggestion, and SignalWatch was born at www.signalwatch.com.

The goal of SignalWatch is to provide technical analysis education for our customers. To fulfill this goal, we provide a number of resources, including market commentary, trading lessons, and daily charts.

Each day, we isolate chart patterns to determine probable direction of the Dow for the next day. SignalWatch is all about charting — learning to identify the key components that make a good opportunity a really great trade. It is through careful isolation of only the best candidates, plus matching the direction of the market, that we beat the odds in our trading.

Why the Dow?

Folks have emailed me asking why I analyze the Dow and not the NASDAQ or S&P. Good question! I use the Dow because it is the best "indicator" of public sentiment I have yet found, though I know it diverges from the NASDAQ quite often. My theory is: "As goes the Dow, so goes the market" because most investors "feel" better or worse based on this "magic" number. And how folks feel is everything.

The stock market is a confidence game, having very little to do with reality or true value (now there's a topic for discussion!). Why else would Amazon trade at an infinite P:E (Price to Earnings) ratio?[6] Or other good stocks be sold down below book value? Investor psychology is the only factor driving prices. Sentiment and the Dow are closely related.

Also, the Dow only has 30 well-followed stocks, primarily traded by institutions. If the Dow gets healthy, that's good for the market. If it tanks, watch out.

---

6 Price to Earnings Ratio is a common measure of stock value. If the price per share is $20 and the stock posts $2 per share in net profits, its P:E ratio is 10 ($20/$2). If there are no earnings, then the formula divides by zero, giving an infinite (and meaningless) P:E ratio.

Consolidations Are Magic!

The best tools for determining overall market trend are consolidations. As we discussed earlier, a consolidation is any sideways or trading range formation that occurs after a significant move. Consolidations almost always indicate the market will continue in the direction of the prior move, and typically will move twice the original distance.

Look at the chart below (See Figure 10-1), on the Dow for 1998. We have marked the various consolidations that were obvious during this time (1, 2, 3, . . .) and measurement points (A, B, C, . . .). The consolidation "1" forecasted a move to "C" because of the distance from "A" to "B" (that is AB ~ BC).

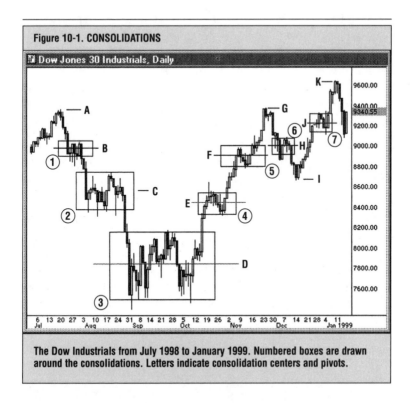

Figure 10-1. CONSOLIDATIONS

The Dow Industrials from July 1998 to January 1999. Numbered boxes are drawn around the consolidations. Letters indicate consolidation centers and pivots.

When consolidation "2" formed, the move from "C" to "D" was likely, because of the distance from "A" to "C" (that is, AC ~ CD).

You can see from the other consolidations on the chart that the next move (continuation in trend) was very predictable from this sort of measurement. Any time you see a consolidation form, ask yourself, "Where is the nearest significant high or low?" Now, measure the same distance in the direction of trend. Seventy percent of the time, a continuation will occur to that price.

In fact, if you measure the distances on the chart between all the consolidation centers and extreme points, you find that distances tend to match:

AB ~ BC   EF ~ FG   AC ~ CD   GH ~ HI   DE ~ EF   IJ ~ JK

Another way to say this is, consolidations measure the 50% point of moves. That is, when you see a consolidation form, you can usually measure the distance to the previous high (or low) and be fairly confident that the market will continue in that direction the same distance. However, consolidations are not perfect. In Figure 10-1 at Consolidation #3, it appeared the market would move down the distance from A-D, or about 600 points. When it broke to the upside to form Consolidation #4, we knew that we had seen a double bottom rather than a consolidation. So, the important rule for consolidations is: "Wait for the breakout."

The consolidation phenomenon repeats itself over and over in charts of all types, including indexes like the Dow, individual stocks, and futures contracts.

What Will the Dow Do Tomorrow?

Remember—nobody can call the market. And that includes me! But we can determine where the forces are. By simply examining the lines of support, resistance, trend and consolidation, we can find levels which, if violated, indicate a particular outcome is probably underway.

If the market appears to be consolidating to the upside, you can measure the distance to the recent low and extrapolate a move of twice the distance, based on consolidation theory. If the market breaks out of the top of the consolidation, your odds of winning on long trades that day or week are tremendously enhanced.

By the same token, if the market approaches an important resistance level and solidly breaks it, you have a good chance of a continued rally twice the distance of the move which led to the top of the resistance.

Finally, if a trendline forms on the Dow, you can look for reversals and breaks. These are often very significant, and lead to beautiful moves in the direction of trend or new trend.

Most often, these patterns work with each other. For example, you may see a trendline form on the upper side of a downward price movement, and then see an ascending line coming up from below. This now forms a consolidation as well as a trendline. Or, you might measure a 38% retracement on the weekly chart and a 62% retracement on the daily. This coincidence of two measurements at the same time is a powerful sign that a reversal is near.

My motto is: "Don't try to predict the Dow. But be ready for a confirmation of direction."

Chapter 11

TRADING THE MOVES
WHILE MINIMIZING RISK

The Golden Exit Rule

Once we take a position with real money in the market, we "become the market" and are subject to the same forces as all other traders, namely fear and greed. This is important to recognize. I can trade someone else's money all day long, and do well. But as soon as I start risking my own funds, something changes. I become fearful of losing. This fear makes me do things that, in hindsight, I realize were wrong decisions. Therefore, I developed The Golden Exit Rule.

> **The Golden Exit Rule**
>
> As soon as your reasons for entering a trade are no longer valid, get out of the position.

Here Are Some Situations That May Invoke The Golden Exit Rule:

• You enter a position because the stock was lagging behind the market. However, the market begins declining as a whole, and appears to be correcting. You see your stock getting hit as well. Get out. Your reason for entering is no longer valid.

• You saw a consolidation on a chart, and entered a long position on a breakout to the upside. However, the stock retraces back into the consolidation, thus proving that it may not have been a consolidation at all, but rather a resistance. Exit that trade!

• You bought stock XYZ because it broke a resistance level. The next few days it trades back through the resistance level and looks weak. Just get out.

We have all fallen victim to the "it will come back" sort of thinking. We don't like admitting we are wrong, but trading is the one pursuit where being wrong is a necessary condition to the activity. It is a game of odds, and what we are trying to do is get the odds in our favor — not delude ourselves into thinking that every event will be a success.

Setting Stops to Minimize Risk

Every time you pull the trigger on a trade, you take the risk of a loss. The good news is, there are some simple techniques you can use to minimize the risk. The most basic of these is the use of stops. A stop is used to exit a position if a certain price level is broken. Generally, they are set below the current market price. In this section, we will discuss how you can use some of the same key patterns to set reasonable stops.

Setting Stops Below Consolidations

Clearly, if a consolidation (trading range) has formed, and you trade the breakout from the consolidation, you can set a stop just below the lower bounds of the consolidation if going long, or the upper bounds if going short.

In the chart below (see Figure 11-1), IBM consolidated for four months — a rather long period of time — before breaking out. (It just so happened, OmniTrader fired a beautiful long signal at the same time.) If we set a stop just below the lower bounds of the consolidation, at about 160, we will know if the breakout was false as soon as price gets to this level. Stops based on consolidation ranges are perhaps the simplest, yet most effective stops available to technical analysts.

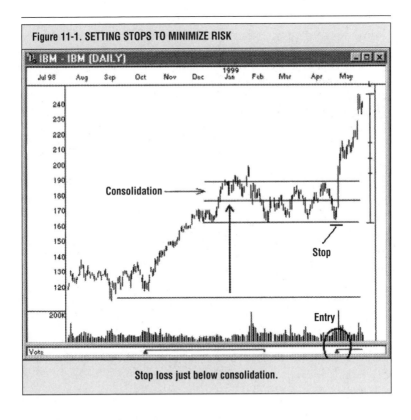

Figure 11-1. SETTING STOPS TO MINIMIZE RISK

Stop loss just below consolidation.

Setting Stops Using Pivot Points

Pivot points are key turning points (reversals) in the market. Pivot points provide a great way to set stops. Basically, if the market trades below (or above) a significant level, we believe it is going to move against a trade and continue lower (or higher, in the case of a short trade).

The chart below (see Figure 11-2) shows pivot point stops chosen for two separate trades. Note that the signal on the left has 15% of price distance down to the lower pivot point, while the trade on the right only has 3%. So, if we use pivot points to set our stop-loss exits, the second trade is clearly superior.

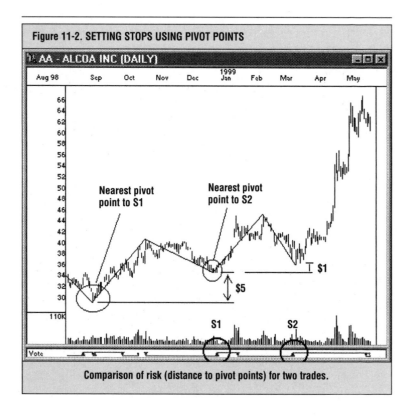

Figure 11-2. SETTING STOPS USING PIVOT POINTS

Comparison of risk (distance to pivot points) for two trades.

Obviously, if you only take trades where your loss risk is 5% to 10%, but your profit potential is 10% to 20%, you only have to be right half the time to do well! That is, if you place ten trades and lose 10% on five, but make 20% on the other five, your net gain is still 5% overall. Of course, our goal is to do better than 50%, but the point is that you should create situations where your gains are larger than your losses. If you do that, you will win.

Maximizing Profits on Every Trade

Clearly, the best place to exit a trade is at the optimal profit level. In this section, we will discuss some methods for determining this exit point (see Table below).

Chart Pattern	Exit Method Applied
Retracement	Look for 38%, 50%, and 62% zones.
Trendlines	Look at projected targets based on parallel lines
Consolidations	Consider any consolidation to mark 50% of the move.

Several chart patterns may be used to formulate exit points.

Retracement Targets

You can define targets based on Fibonacci retracement levels of 38%, 50%, and 62% (see Figure 11-3). Particularly in markets that oscillate and form "waves," this can be a powerful exit technique.

Set your exit point at the next retracement level. If price barrels through the level you have set, then set it at the next level and set an exit stop at the prior level.

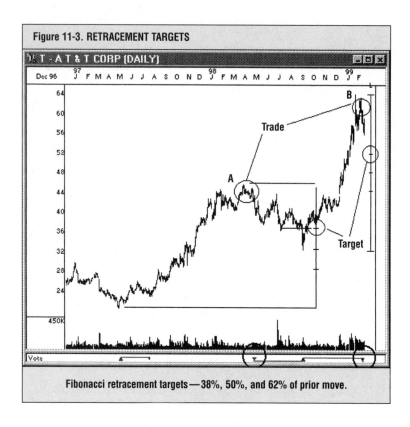

Figure 11-3. RETRACEMENT TARGETS

Fibonacci retracement targets — 38%, 50%, and 62% of prior move.

To illustrate this point, look again at Figure 11-3. After going short at point "A," we waited until price moved through a retracement level, and then exited on the reversal.

Parallel Trendline Targets

When you have a defined trendline (see Figure 11-4), you can draw another trendline above it to form a channel. This higher line (imaginary parallel trendline) is your target for exiting the trade.

Visually check to see if price is approaching an upper trendline in the case of a long, or a lower trendline in the case of a short. As these key reversal points are hit, the market will

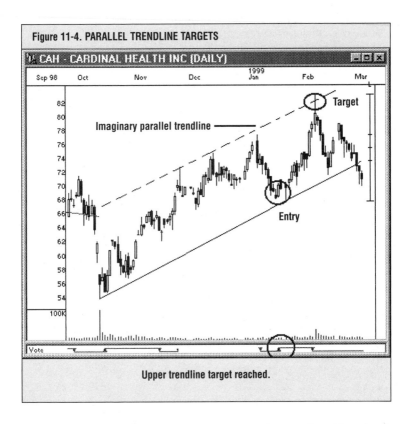

Figure 11-4. PARALLEL TRENDLINE TARGETS

CAH - CARDINAL HEALTH INC (DAILY)

Imaginary parallel trendline

Target

Entry

Upper trendline target reached.

be more vulnerable to a correction, and you should tighten your stops.

Consolidation Targets

The fourth exhaustion pattern, the consolidation target, also deserves some discussion. Remember from our discussion earlier, we pointed out how well consolidations mark the 50% points of moves. Obviously, if consolidations measure the 50% point, we can tell when to get out by looking at the double point.

Using our previous example of IBM, the chart on the next page (see Figure 11-5) shows a trade we entered on the back

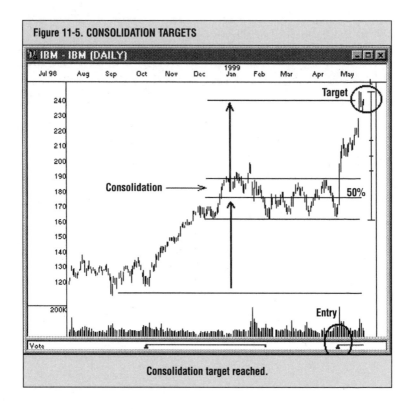

Figure 11-5. CONSOLIDATION TARGETS

IBM - IBM (DAILY)

Target

Consolidation

50%

Entry

Consolidation target reached.

side of a consolidation (on the breakout). Now, we are sitting at the 2x (double) point target, and should tighten stops in anticipation of an exit.

Put the Odds in Your Favor!

Whenever you consider placing a trade, look at your stop loss and profit target. Try to achieve a reward:risk point that is at least 2:1 on any trade. That is, the perceived reward distance should be 2 times the stop level.

The table below shows four hypothetical trades that yielded a 2% daily gain, even though only half of the trades were successful. Note also that the gains are not quite twice the losses.

Trade #	G/L on Trade	G/L on Account
1	+10%	+2.5%
2	+9%	+2.25%
3	-5%	-1.25%
4	-6%	-1.5%
Total	**+8%**	**+2.0%**

Average daily gain of +2% on four day trades.

Clearly, you will expect to be more than 50% correct in your trading, but by always trying to select candidates that exhibit stop and target levels consistent with a 2:1 ratio, you are ahead of the game and have a good chance of meeting our 2% per day requirement.

▲ ▲ ▲ ▲ ▲ ▲

Closing Thoughts . . .

C hart patterns form because people react to price movements in consistent ways based mostly on fear, greed, and herd mentality. Knowing this, we can then focus our attention on chart pattern formations and take advantage of the resulting opportunities including those detailed in this book.

"A stock is never so low that it can't go lower, nor so high it can't go higher."
— Edwin LeFevre, *Reminiscences of a Stock Operator*

"The key to being successful as a trader is not losing money in between the big moves, but staying in the market so you are there when the big move comes."
— *Wise Trader* (Anonymous)

"You only need ONE pattern to be successful."
— Linda Bradford Raschke, *Market Wizard*

One percent a day is all you need!
Good luck in your quest . . .

Trading
Resource
Guide

▲ ▲ ▲ ▲ ▲ ▲

TOOLS FOR SUCCESS
IN TRADING

Trading Resource Guide

The Encyclopedia of Chart Patterns

by Thomas N. Bulkowski

Brand new comprehensive guide covers chart formations, identifies chart patterns, explains market behavior, and provides up-to-date performance statistics on which patterns presage different market events.

$85.00 Item #BC100x-10781

Point and Figure Charting: The Essential Application for Forecasting and Tracking Market Prices, 2nd Edition

by Thomas J. Dorsey

This brand new second edition is out - updated to show new and experienced investors alike how to bring charting into the internet age. You'll discover cutting-edge new techniques to help you create, maintain, and interpret your own Point & Figure charts. Use your findings to track and forecast market prices and to develop an overall investment strategy. This book will help you boost your confidence in the market and take decisive action at the appropriate time, rather than reacting after the fact.

$59.95 Item# BC100x-12204

▲ ▲ ▲ ▲ ▲ ▲

Many of these books, along with hundreds of others, are available at a discount from Traders' Library.
To place an order, or find out more, visit us at

www.traderslibrary.com

or call us at

1-800-272-2855.

How Charts Can Help You In the Stock Market

by William L. Jiler

Standard & Poor's Press brings impressive knowledge and resources to some of today's most challenging financial issues. Covering subjects from saving for college to technical analysis to risk management, books in the series will give both independent and institutional investors the knowledge they need to dramatically improve their overall financial decisions. The classic primer on technical analysis, reprinted for a new generation of traders and technicians.

$19.95   Item #BC100x-1661720

Technical Analysis Simplified

by Clif Droke

Here's a concise, easy-reading manual for learning and implementing this invaluable investment tool. The author distills the most essential elements of technical analysis into a brief, easy-to-read volume. Droke's compact guide is a great starting place — and the perfect complement to any technical analysis software program.

$29.95   Item #BC100x-11087

Trader's Guide to Technical Analysis

by C. Colburn Hardy

Achieving high-impact results can be made easier by implementing the most effective technical analysis tools throughout your trading day. In this easy-to-read classic, you will learn when to buy and sell stocks with the help of technical analysis — written for the average investor.

You will also learn to recognize trends and pinpoint entry points, and how to improve trading results by combining technical and fundamental tools and techniques.

$37.50   Item #BC100x-11563

Charting Made Easy

by John J. Murphy

Renowned market technician John Murphy presents basic principles of chart reading in easy-to-understand terms. In the book he covers all types of chart analysis, "need to know" concepts such as trend lines, moving averages, reversal patterns, price gaps, price patterns and more.

This book will also teach you how to use the industry's top tools to obtain a better understanding of what charts can do — and how they can help you grab your portion of today's trading profits.

$19.95 Item #BC100x-11353

Martin Pring's Introduction to Technical Analysis, A CD-Rom Seminar and Workbook

by Martin J. Pring

The foremost expert on technical analysis and forecasting financial markets gives you a one-on-one course in every aspect of technical analysis. This interactive guide explains how to evaluate trends, highs and lows, price/volume relationships, price patterns, moving averages, and momentum indicators.

The CD-Rom includes videos, animated diagrams, audio clips, and interactive tests. It's the user-friendly way to master technical analysis from an industry icon.

$49.95 Item #BC100x-8521

▲ ▲ ▲ ▲ ▲ ▲

To place an order, or find out more, visit us at

www.traderslibrary.com

or call us at

1-800-272-2855.

Profits in Volume: Equivolume Charting

by Richard Arms

This method places emphasis on the trading range and trading volume - which are considered to be the two primary factors involved in technical analysis. They give an accurate appraisal of the supply/demand factors that influence a stock. Once you know this critical factor, you can determine if a stock is moving with ease or difficulty.

$39.95   Item# BC100x-6780

Bar Chart Basics

by Darrell R. Jobman

Bar charts are the most popular method for identifying market turning points. Now, this compact guide explains bar charts in terms anyone can understand. For beginners, it's the first step in your technical analysis course of study; for experienced investors, it's a great way to review — and profit from — the basics.

$19.95 Item #BC100x-10095

Technical Analysis for the Trading Professional

by Constance Brown

New technical traders, armed with plug-and-play technical software and Internet access are forcing traders to adopt radical new uses and combinations of indicators and formulas to retain a competitive edge. Now, never seen before formulas are presented by a top technical expert.

Innovative and accurate — and not for the novice — this new work can make your analysis and your trading more effective.

$49.95 Item #BC100x-10544

Mastering Technical Analysis

by Michael C. Thomsett

In an era of unassisted Internet investing, this new book makes available — and simplifies — the tools professionals use to profit in the market. The key to technical analysis is to interpret and incorporate technical indicators into your own investment program. Now, Thomsett shows you how to gather information, sift through it, and make informed decisions about the market based on a variety of indicators — so you can go the distance to earning solid, consistent gains.

$27.00   Item #BC100x-10717

Technical Analysis of Stock Trends, 8th Edition

by Edwards and Magee

The universally acclaimed investor's classic has now been updated with the latest data and references. With more than 800,000 copies in previous editions, this is the definitive reference on analyzing trends in stock performance. It incorporates the most recent stock information and updated charts for expert guidance.

$99.95   Item #BC100x-17379

▲ ▲ ▲ ▲ ▲ ▲

Elliott Wave Simplified

by Clif Droke

Now a noted market technician takes the mystery out of this effective technique — without deluging readers with details. Find the basics of technical analysis and R.N. Elliott's simple and proven theory, plus pitfalls most practitioners make. Also, discover how the theory relates to trading volume, contrary opinion, channel analysis, the fan principle, filtered waves and other often overlooked aspects. Get proven methods to determine the current and future condition of any given stock — in simple, easy-to-grasp terms.

$29.95 Item #BC100x-11054.

Dynamic Trading Indicators: Winning with Value Charts and Price Action Profile

by Mark W. Helweg and David Stendahl

Get a thorough overview of two innovative market analysis tools, Value Charts and Price Action Profile, and discover how to use them to trade all markets with confidence. Expert advice, real-world examples, and crystal clear charts help you to develop systems and trading programs that work. Not all charting techniques are created equal. Understand two of the most revolutionary trading indicators currently available - and unlock the door to unlimited profits.

$69.95 Item# BC100x-84583

▲ ▲ ▲ ▲ ▲ ▲

To place an order, or find out more, visit us at

www.traderslibrary.com

or call us at

1-800-272-2855.

Suggested DVD Training Courses

Strategies for Profiting with Japanese Candlestick Charts

by Steve Nison

What are Japanese Candlesticks and why should traders use them? This brand new video workshop will help you understand and master this powerful tool with high impact results. Steve Nison is the premiere expert on Candlesticks in the world, and now you can benefit from his expertise in the comfort of your own home.

$695.00   DVD Item# BC100x-2434165

Mastering High Probability Chart Reading Methods

by John Murphy

Post big gains - even if the market is locked in a downward spiral - by following the powerful sector trading strategies of renowned technical analyst John Murphy. The Traders Hall of Fame honoree shows you step-by-step how to pinpoint the right sectors to play at the right time - and how to shift seamlessly from one to the other - with profits in tow. Citing key relationships among markets - from stocks to commodities, bonds to currencies - Murphy's methods help you determine when to move from one to the other so you're poised to capture the most lucrative opportunities available in any market climate.

$99.00   DVD Item# BC100x-3309702

Using Option Charts to Boost Trading Profits

by Price Headley

Discover powerful new charting techniques for selecting optimum entry and exit points that can exponentially boost your trading profits and limit your risk exposure. Join BigTrends.com founder and best selling author Price Headley, as he outlines a systematic new approach to option analysis that's winning raves from professional and active traders alike. In easy to understand language - and with a full online support manual as a guide - Headley highlights the elements that make his new approach to trading options one of the most practical and most popular around. Find out why traders are raving, "This is one workshop that was not just worth my money - but my time!"

$99.00   DVD Item# BC100x-982788

▲ ▲ ▲ ▲ ▲ ▲

To place an order, or find out more, visit us at
www.traderslibrary.com
or call us at
1-800-272-2855.

Important Internet Sites

Traders' Library Bookstore . . . **www.traderslibrary.com**
The #1 source for trading and investment books, videos, audios, and software.

OmniTrader . . . . **www.omnitrader.com**
Learn more about how OmniTrader software can help you win in the markets, whether you are a short- or long-term trader.

Martin Pring . . . . **www.optionstrategist.com**
This site is dedicated to teaching the art of technical analysis and charting.

Elliott Wave International . . . . **www.elliottwave.com**
A premier source of technical analysis information.

Newsletters of Interest to Traders

SignalWatch
Editor, Ed Downs
www.signalwatch.com

Dow Theory Letters
Editor, Richard Russell
www.dowtheoryletters.com

Daily Option Strategist
Editor, Larry McMillan
www.optionstrategist.com

Option Advisor
Editor, Bernie Schaffer
www.optionadvisor.com

Option Strategist
Editor, Larry McMillan
www.optionstrategist.com

Stock Market Cycles
Editor, Peter Eliades
www.stockmarketcycles.com

About OmniTrader Software

▲ ▲ ▲ ▲ ▲ ▲

More self-directed traders and individual investors are choosing OmniTrader™ 2000 for several good reasons . . .

1 This revolutionary new software AUTOMATES much of the trading process — so your computer does the heavy-lifting analysis, instead of you doing all the research.

2 OmniTrader 2000 ADAPTS to changing markets, and generates "consensus" buy and sell signals for you to review. Whether the market is up or down, you'll have a list of good candidates to trade.

3 Plus, OmniTrader 2000 EDUCATES you on how to be a better trader. You'll learn how to use Technical Analysis and charts more effectively in your trading.

Here's How OmniTrader 2000 Works . . .

FOR TRADING:

- **Stocks**
- **Indexes**
- **Mutual Funds**
- **Futures and**
- **Options**

First, OmniTrader 2000 automatically tests up to 120 built-in trading systems on each symbol in your list. That's right — you don't have to develop systems from scratch like you do with other programs. Then using its exclusive Adaptive Reasoning Model™ (ARM), OmniTrader 2000 selects only the top performing systems to generate "consensus" buy and sell signals for you to review. So no matter what the markets are doing (trending up/down, trading within a range, or acting very volatile), OmniTrader 2000 adapts to give you a list of great candidates to review.

OmniTrader 2000 also provides the relevant information you need to confirm signals and isolate the BEST candidates to trade. Pull up charts with trendlines, support & resistance levels, and more automatically plotted for you. Click on "OT Online" each day to learn the likely direction of the overall market, which industry groups to watch for rotations, and receive lessons on how to interpret charts more effectively in your trading.

SUPPORTED DATA FORMATS:

- **TC2000**
- **Telescan**
- **eSignal**
- **InterQuote**
- **Quote.com**
- **and many more!**

Once you've made a trade, OmniTrader 2000's built-in Portfolio Manager helps you manage your orders, stops and positions with real time alerts. There are even trading simulators to help improve your trading skills and confidence with the product without risking your money in the market.

Whether you hold positions for minutes, days, weeks or months, OmniTrader 2000 can help you win in the markets.

To Order Omni Trader Call:

1-800-272-2855 or 410-964-0026
Item #BC100-7122 (Stocks Edition)
Item #BC100-7123 (Futures Edition)
Order Online: www.traderslibrary.com

SPECIAL OFFER
$50 OFF

Mention special offer code TLXX1 and receive $50.00 off the retail price of OmniTrader 2000! Time is running out — contact us today!

Free 2 Week Trial Offer for U.S. Residents From Investor's Business Daily:

INVESTOR'S BUSINESS DAILY will provide you with the facts, figures, and objective news analysis you need to succeed.

Investor's Business Daily is formatted for a quick and concise read to help you make informed and profitable decisions.

To take advantage of this free 2 week trial offer, e-mail us at customerservice@traderslibrary.com or visit our website at www.traderslibrary.com where you find other free offers as well.

You can also reach us by calling 1-800-272-2855 or fax us at 410-964-0027.

About the Author

▲ ▲ ▲ ▲ ▲ ▲

A 20-year veteran of trading, Ed Downs is the developer of the OmniTrader software, which was released in 1994. Now in its fifth version, OmniTrader is recognized around the world as one of the leaders in trading system automation.

Downs is also the editor of the SignalWatch daily market column, where he evaluates the overall market, provides trading lessons, and selects charts that are exhibiting proven technical analysis patterns. The column can be viewed at www.signalwatch.com.

Downs has a B.S. degree in Mechanical Engineering from the University of Texas and a M.S. degree in Electrical Engineering also from the University of Texas. Well versed in engineering theory and practice, Downs has successfully applied automation principles to trading through the development of OmniTrader.

This book, along with other books, is available at discounts that make it realistic to provide it as a gift to your customers, clients, and staff. For more information on these long-lasting, cost-effective premiums, please call us at 800-272-2855 or e-mail us at sales@traderslibrary.com.